This book is
for Stella so that
she may learn about
her Oklahoma heritage.

Love,
Lola Shaw
6-4-11

S is for Sooner

An Oklahoma Alphabet

Written by Devin Scillian and Illustrated by Kandy Radzinski

Sleeping Bear Press™
310 North Main Street, Suite 300
Chelsea, MI 48118
www.sleepingbearpress.com

© 2003 Sleeping Bear Press is an imprint of Gale, a part of Cengage Learning.

Printed and bound in the United States.

10 9 8 7 6 5 4

Library of Congress Cataloging-in-Publication Data
Scillian, Devin.
S is for Sooner : an Oklahoma alphabet / written by Devin Scillian ;
illustrated by Kandy Radzinski.
p. cm.
Summary: The letters of the alphabet are represented by words, set in short
rhymes with additional information, relating to the state of Oklahoma.
ISBN 978-1-58536-062-8
1. Oklahoma-Juvenile literature. 2. English language-Alphabet-Juvenile
literature. [1. Oklahoma. 2. Alphabet.] I. Radzinski, Kandy, ill. II. Title.
F694.3 .S297 2003
976.6—dc22   2003015308

For Mike and Burns, two dear friends
and two great Oklahomans.

DEVIN

∾

To my Mom, Lee Williams, who said to me over and over again:
"You can grow up to be anything you want to be."

And to my family at Tulsa Christian Fellowship.

KANDY

OK, we're ready. OK, let's go.
We're all OK, and by now you know,
we come from Oklahoma
where prairie dogs play.
And where buffalo pound their hooves
in the dark red clay.

Impressed with the written language of the European settlers who came to America, a young Cherokee named Sequoyah dreamed of a written language for his own people. He counted 85 different sounds in the Cherokee language and created characters for each one. He called them "talking leaves," and when you think about it, words written on a piece of paper are like leaves that talk. After creating his alphabet, Sequoyah came to Oklahoma from Arkansas and became a leader of the Western Cherokee.

A is for the alphabet of the American Cherokee
invented by Sequoyah, who taught the tribe to read.
He knew that one who reads and writes is one who best achieves.
So he gave his people a lasting gift, his powerful "talking leaves."

A a

B is for the bravery of the Buffalo Soldier men.
They saved the territory from cutthroats and knaves.
But they were different for their day, the sons of former slaves.

B Sit by my side a second. A moment we should spend.

The history of African-Americans in Oklahoma is unlike that of any other state. They came to Oklahoma as settlers, farmers, cowboys, and soldiers. Black soldiers built Oklahoma forts and protected the frontier from cattle thieves and rogues. The bravery of these soldiers so impressed the Indian tribes in the region that they began calling them "Buffalo Soldiers."

After the Civil War, the state became known as a place where black settlers could lead free and productive lives. In time, Oklahoma had more predominantly black towns and cities than the rest of the country put together.

B is also for Beaver's Bend State Park in southeastern Oklahoma. Vacationers love its crystal clear lakes and rivers and 100-foot-tall pine trees.

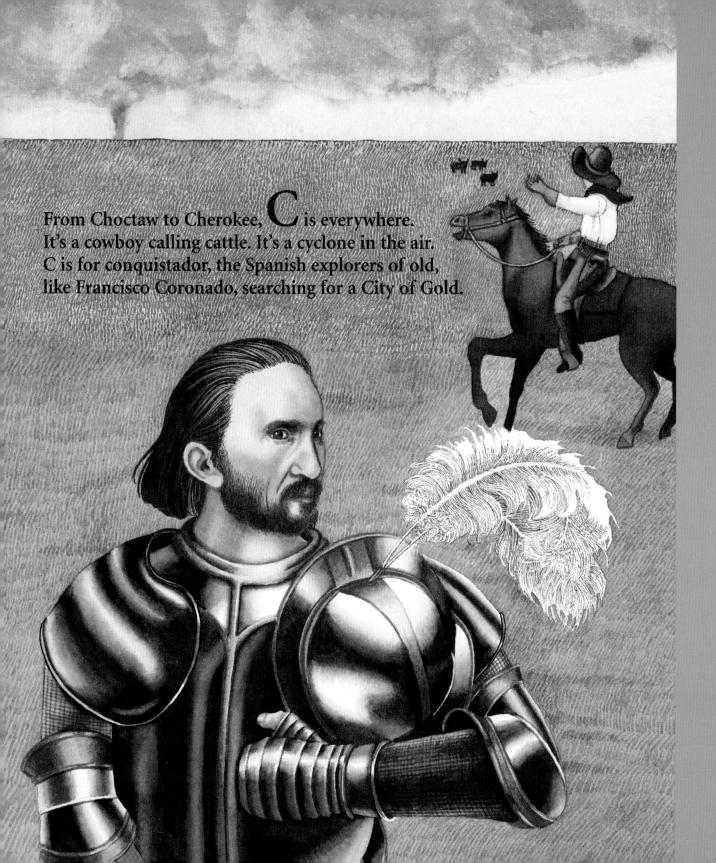

From Choctaw to Cherokee, C is everywhere.
It's a cowboy calling cattle. It's a cyclone in the air.
C is for conquistador, the Spanish explorers of old,
like Francisco Coronado, searching for a City of Gold.

Francisco Vasquez de Coronado was among the first Europeans to explore the area that would come to be known as Oklahoma. He arrived in 1541, marking the beginning of Oklahoma's recorded history.

In the late 1800s, cowboys moved enormous herds of cattle from Texas through Oklahoma to Kansas. During the trail-drive days, six million cattle traveled the Chisholm Trail through Oklahoma. The National Cowboy Hall of Fame is located in Oklahoma City and it continues to celebrate the cowboy heritage of the Old West.

A cyclone is another name for a tornado. It can also be called a twister.

D is the dunes of Little Sahara. It's a drive down Route 66.
It's the Dust Bowl drought, dreary and dry, which *The Grapes of Wrath* depicts.
And D is for detective. Dick Tracy is never fooled.
Dashing and daring and drawn with the pen of the artist Chester Gould.

The sand dunes of Little Sahara State Park near Waynoka are actually growing. The dunes stretch another foot toward the northwest every year. Route 66 is one of the most legendary highways in American history. It runs from Chicago, Illinois, to Los Angeles, California, and stretches across 400 miles of Oklahoma.

In the 1930s the combination of severe drought and bad farming practices devastated the southern Great Plains. Oklahoma was one of the parched states that became known as the "Dust Bowl." John Steinbeck immortalized the drought and its victims in his classic novel *The Grapes of Wrath*.

Chester Gould was born in Pawnee in 1900. His brilliant comic-strip detective "Dick Tracy" made his debut in newspapers in 1931. Even though Gould died in 1985, other cartoonists have carried on his work and Dick Tracy is still solving crimes in the comics section today.

Enid and Elk City. E is either of those.
There's El Reno and Edmond and Eskimo Joe's.
It's the edge of an embankment, where an eagle eyes a snake.
It's evening at Lake Eufaula, Oklahoma's biggest lake.

Oklahoma can be a perfect place to see our national symbol, the bald eagle. Many of the eagles that spend their summers in the northern United States make their winter home in the trees that line the waterways of Oklahoma.

Oklahoma has more man-made lakes than any other state. There are more than 200, adding up to 2,000 miles of shoreline. Six hundred of those miles are found on Lake Eufaula. Due to the red soil, the northern part of the lake has a pinkish hue, but it turns a clear blue as you head south.

Eskimo Joe's is a restaurant in Stillwater. Its T-shirts have become so popular you may see the smiling Eskimo Joe and his dog Buffy just about any-where in the world.

Oklahoma's forts are testimony to the complicated nature of Oklahoma's history. The Oklahoma story is a tug-of-war between white settlers and pioneers and Native Americans who were stripped of their goods and land. The pioneering spirit helped create the Oklahoma that exists today but at a great cost to the people who lived here long before the first European explorers arrived.

Military forts are still important to Oklahoma. Oklahoma is home to three Air Force bases (Tinker, Vance, and Altus) and one Army base (Ft. Sill).

They call it "bedlam" when the University of Oklahoma Sooners play against the Oklahoma State University Cowboys. OU is in Norman. OSU is in Stillwater.

Follow F. You'll find four forts under the frontier sky:
Ft. Sill, Ft. Cobb, Ft. Gibson, too, and also Ft. Supply.
And F stands for football and a fan's favorite day
when the Sooners and the Cowboys take the field and play.

FORT GIBSON
COMMANDING
OFFICERS
QUARTERS

Get along to Gage, or Guymon way out west.
For a glimpse of gorgeous gables you may like Guthrie best.
And **G** is for Geronimo who had a courage so rare
that parachutists call his name when they jump into the air.

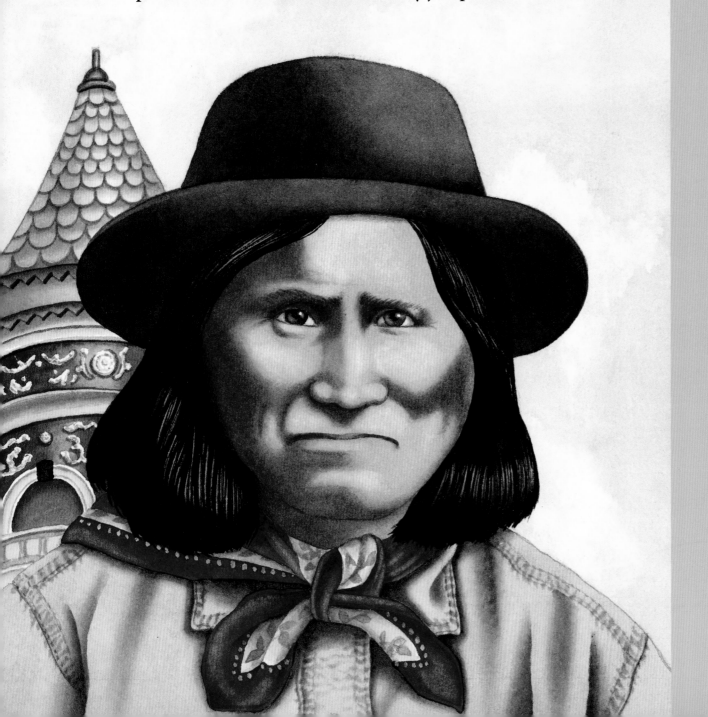

G g

Geronimo was a fierce Apache warrior. Pioneers and settlers feared him as a murderer, but many have come to see Geronimo as a brave leader who fought against all that was being taken from his people. He was one of the last Indian warriors to surrender to the United States. He lived the last years of his life at Ft. Sill and was buried at the Apache cemetery there in 1909.

The beautiful Victorian town of Guthrie was Oklahoma's first capital, but a vote of the people moved the capital south to Oklahoma City. Gables are the decorative peaks found on the sloping rooftops of many of the old homes in Guthrie.

H is Oscar Hammerstein, who helped Richard Rodgers create
the musical *Oklahoma,* a play about our state.
    And H is hospitality everywhere you go,
from a Henryetta "Howdy" to a Hennessey "Hello."

Oklahoma is one of the most beloved musicals of all time. Written in 1943 it was the first musical written by the team of Rodgers and Hammerstein. They based the play on "Green Grow the Lilacs," a story about life in Oklahoma written by Lynn Riggs. The title song was so popular with Oklahomans that it became the official state song in 1953.

Oklahoma has the largest Native American population of any state in the United States. Members of 67 different tribes call Oklahoma home. Many Native Americans continue to honor the traditions and rituals handed down from generation to generation.

Today those who enjoy the beauty of Native American customs and ceremonies attend the Red Earth Festival in Oklahoma City, the largest arts event of its kind.

Okla means "people" and *humma* means "red." They're the Choctaw words that give our state its name.

Imagine the American Indian, an impressive image indeed.
Wearing an imperial headdress, on the back of an imposing steed.
Intricate and important, their ceremonies inspire
with a flourish of colorful feathers and the crackle of cleansing fire.

J j

J is for the James Gang, brothers Jesse and Frank,
jubilant with the jackpot they just stole from a bank.
Neither judge nor jury nor jailer could keep them in a cage.
Some say Jesse faked his death and lived to a ripe old age.

Jesse James is one of the most notorious outlaws in American history and a powerful presence in Oklahoma folklore. He and his brother Frank were born in Missouri. Shortly after the Civil War, Jesse and Frank began robbing banks and trains, outrunning the law and escaping from prison along the way.

A man named Bob Ford killed Jesse James in St. Joseph, Missouri in 1882. But for more than 50 years rumors persisted that Jesse was alive and well and living in Oklahoma. Occasionally an Oklahoman would actually claim to be Jesse. And some still insist that Jesse managed to live to the ripe old age of 104.

We do know that Frank spent most of the rest of his life on an Oklahoma farm until his death in 1915.

You'll think I'm kidding about letter K, but get your appetite ready. We're off to Krebs for plates of lasagna, meatballs, and spaghetti.
It's not cowboy grub, but just breathe in that tasty Italian aroma, a piece of Italy tucked away in southeast Oklahoma.

In the 1800s many Italian immigrants made their way to Krebs in southwestern Oklahoma to work in the area's coal mines. As the coal mine era faded, displaced miners started to open restaurants and groceries specializing in the foods of their Italian homeland. Those flavors remain today in area restaurants and especially in Lovera's Grocery, which sells homemade Italian sausages and cheeses.

Krebs is near McAlester, which holds its Italian Festival every spring. It's one of the biggest celebrations in the state.

L is for Shannon Lucid, lifting off with grace.
    She reminds us Oklahoma has put many into space.
Growing up in Oklahoma, you can dream of riding high
    through the wide and endless span of the Oklahoma sky.

Shannon Lucid has spent more time in orbit than any woman in the world. She's the only woman to be awarded the Congressional Space Medal of Honor by the president of the United States.

Oklahoma has produced many astronauts. They include Gordon Cooper, who was one of the original *Mercury Seven* astronauts and was the first man to fly two orbits around the earth.

Thomas Stafford made four space flights, including *Apollo 10*.

Other Oklahoma astronauts include Stuart Roosa, Owen Garriott, William Pogue, and John Harrington.

Ll

A medley of music makes us move from Muskogee to Meeker to Meers.
Country music can make you merry or move you right to tears.
M The state flower begins with M and makes a merrier me.
M is marvelous mistletoe, which grows in the top of a tree.

Oklahoma has a special place in the history of country music. Among the many influential singers and musicians with Oklahoma ties are Woody Guthrie, Roy Clark, Jimmy Webb, Sandi Patty, Reba McEntire, Vince Gill, Garth Brooks, Joe Diffie, and Toby Keith. Other kinds of music have also been given an Oklahoma flavor from entertainers like Leon Russell, B.J. Thomas, and Hanson.

Mistletoe is the official state flower of Oklahoma. It's the oldest of Oklahoma's symbols, adopted in 1893, 14 years before Oklahoma was even a state.

Mistletoe grows in the tops of hardwood trees. Always prized at Christmastime, it is very difficult to reach by hand. Often, it's shot out of a treetop with a shotgun.

M m

N is a nice way to help us remember
that in 1907 in the month of November,
from Norman to Nowata, a need to celebrate
a new Oklahoma, our 46th state.

The road to statehood was very long
and difficult for Oklahoma. The first
proposal for Oklahoma statehood came
in 1893. But there were great debates
about whether Indian Territory should
be included in the new state of Oklahoma.
In 1905, the leaders of Indian Territory
met in Muskogee and adopted a plan
to create their own state to be called
Sequoyah, but the United States Congress
never acted on the proposal. It became
clear to many that only a united
Oklahoma could receive statehood, and
in 1906, President Theodore Roosevelt
approved the plan that would make
Oklahoma the 46th state in the U.S.A.

Oklahoma City or OKC.
Say it either way, it's okay by me. O stands for oil,
Of course in Oklahoma, O stands for oil,
oozing from an oil well in the Oklahoma soil.

Oil is one of the most important resources in the world. So it was quite a day in April 15, 1897 when oil started to gush from a huge oil well near Bartlesville. The well was on the property of Cherokee citizen Nellie Johnstone, and thus the well was nick-named "Nellie Johnstone No. 1." It became the state's first truly success-ful oil well. In no time at all, people were coming from all over the world seeking their fortune in Oklahoma.

Oklahoma is the only state in the country with a working oil well on the grounds of its state capitol.

P is for panhandle. Our state looks that way.
    But it didn't always have the kind of shape it has today.
Three Texas counties became Oklahoma land.
    And they made a perfect handle for Oklahoma's pan.

CIMARRON TEXAS BEAVER

Scissor-tailed Flycatcher
State bird of Oklahoma

In 1850 the state of Texas handed a vast area of land to the U.S. government. Most of it was divided into other states, but for 40 years the rectangle that would become the Oklahoma panhandle sat unattached to any state or territory. It became known as "No Man's Land."

Finally, in 1890, the strip of land was declared part of Oklahoma Territory. By 1907 it was divided into Beaver, Texas, and Cimarron counties.

Cimarron County borders more states than any other United States county (Texas, Kansas, Colorado, and New Mexico).

Pp

A quick little quip in the quest for letter Q.
The towns of Quinlan, Quinton, and Quapaw will do.
And a big Q for Quartz Mountain. When the day is done,
it glitters like a pile of diamonds in the sun.

Rock climbers are drawn to the huge fields of granite boulders and rock formations at Quartz Mountain Nature Park near Altus.

Quapaw in northeastern Oklahoma is the tribal headquarters for the Quapaw Tribe. Quapaw means "downstream people."

The town of Quinton is named for Elizabeth Jacob Quinton, who is believed to have been 115 years old when she died in 1941.

Will Rogers was one of the most beloved Americans in history. He was many things—a trick roper, a newspaper writer, a radio commentator, a movie star, and a philosopher. Born in the Indian Nation near Oolagah in 1879, he became an expert with a lasso and began performing in Wild West shows. Soon he began telling jokes, and his keen and humorous observations on life and politics became legendary. He loved people and once said, "I never met a man I didn't like."

Oklahoma rodeos have created some of the greatest riders and rodeo cowboys of all time. They include Bill Pickett, who invented steer wrestling (known then as bulldogging).

R r

A rip-roaring roundup for a rowdy rodeo,
ready for a ride, and roping on the go.
And R is for Will Rogers, Oklahoma's clown prince,
with his Oklahoma wit and uncommon common sense.

On April 22, 1889, a cannon was fired at noon as the signal to start the Land Run. Settlers poured in on foot, on horseback, and in covered wagons to claim a piece of land. By the end of that first day, nearly 10,000 people had settled in Oklahoma City. The people who took part in the Land Run came to be known as "89ers." Those who snuck in early were known as "Sooners."

S s

"So what's a Sooner?" you may ask. Well, in 1889, settlers waited for the signal to leave the starting line. They raced to claim their land without a boundary or fence. Some were sooner than others, and they've been Sooners ever since.

Tt

Starting in the 1820s the United States government forced many Native Americans to leave their homes to live in Indian Territory (which would later become Oklahoma). Tulsa was founded in 1836 by Creek Indians who built a settlement around the Council Oak tree, which still stands today.

The move to Indian Territory was a sad and tragic journey for many. The Cherokee people in particular were put through terrible hardships, making their way to Oklahoma during a cold and bitter winter. Many of them died and were buried along the journey, and thus it became known as "The Trail of Tears."

T is time for Tulsa, and its towers tall and trim.
Or take a trip to Lake Texoma and tumble in for a swim.
It's Turner Falls and Tahlequah and T still remains
The Trail of Tears that led so many to the Oklahoma plains.

U stands for "uh-oh," a most unlikely blunder
when Boise City found the wrong airplane to be under.
An unaware pilot unsure of what to do
hit the only town in America bombed in World War Two.

Just after midnight on July 5, 1943, a B-17 bomber from Dalhart Army Air Base was on a practice mission. The plane was supposed to drop its bombs on a practice range in Texas about 30 miles south of Boise City. The plane veered way off course and mistook the lights of Boise City for the lights of the practice range. Six 96-pound sand bag "bombs" were dropped on the city. Luckily, they did little damage and no one was hurt.

U u

V

V is for the victories Oklahoma's heroes won.
It's Shannon Miller at the Olympics. It's a Mickey Mantle home run.
It's the valor of Wiley Post, a pioneer in aviation.
It's the vision of Wilma Mankiller, Chief of the Cherokee Nation.

With seven Olympic medals and nine World Championship medals, Shannon Miller of Edmond is the most decorated American gymnast in history.

Mickey Mantle grew up playing baseball in Commerce and went on to become one of the greatest players of all time. Known as "The Mick" when he played with the New York Yankees, he hit 536 home runs.

In 1933, Wiley Post became the first person ever to complete a solo flight around the world. He and Will Rogers were killed in a plane crash in Alaska in 1935.

Born in Tahlequah, Wilma Mankiller made history when she became the first woman in modern history to lead a major Native American tribe.

The sky can go from lovely blue to something rather scary.
So **W** stands for weather, which can be extraordinary.
For the weather here can change in the blink of a prairie eye.
When the western winds start whirling, keep one eye on the sky.

Oklahoma's weather can be a wild mixture of extremes. Ranchers and others who work outdoors learn to watch the sky for storms that can come out of nowhere.

Tornadoes are fairly common in Oklahoma. In fact, per square mile, there are more tornadoes in Oklahoma than any other state. These violent, whirling winds can reach speeds of 500 miles an hour, strong enough to blow over cars and buildings and destroy entire towns. But most Oklahomans learn about tornado safety at an early age and know just what to do if they hear a tornado siren.

W
W

On April 19th, 1995, a huge explosion destroyed the Alfred P. Murrah Federal Building in downtown Oklahoma City. One hundred sixty-seven men, women, and children were killed in the terrible blast. A young man named Timothy McVeigh caused the explosion because he was angry with the United States government. But for many, the tragedy was not a lesson in anger, but one of love. Workers came from all over to help in the rescue. People from all over the world sent packages, supplies, and messages and tokens of love and sympathy. A beautiful memorial now stands where the Murrah Building once stood, reminding all of the power of human kindness.

Put an X on the calendar every April nineteen,
For both the saddest and the proudest day we've ever seen.
Lives were lost and lives were changed in the smoke and dusty air.
But the entire world came running just to show they care.
So put an X on the calendar. Always remember the date
when Oklahoma taught the world that love is stronger than hate.

Y y

Give a yell! Yahoo for Yale, a fine town we say.
It was the home of young Jim Thorpe, the best athlete of his day.
And yippee-yay for Yukon, where flour is milled for cooks.
And where good old country music found a star in Garth Brooks.

Many believe that Jim Thorpe was the greatest American athlete of all time. Thorpe was a Native American of the Sac and Fox tribe. He played both professional baseball and football, and as a track star, won two Olympic gold medals in 1912.

With his energetic concerts and rollicking country songs, Garth Brooks revolutionized country music. With more than 100 million albums sold, Garth is the most successful solo recording artist in music history. He was born in Tulsa, but raised in Yukon just outside Oklahoma City.

Yukon is home to the "Yukon's Best" flour mill.

The Arbuckle Wilderness is tucked into the Arbuckle Mountains between Oklahoma City and the Texas state line. It's filled with exotic animals like rhinos, tigers, lions, cougars, giraffes, and, of course, zebras. The Arbuckle Mountains are thought to be among the oldest mountains on earth.

In 1806 Lt. Zebulon Pike was sent to explore the Great Plains and the Rocky Mountains. He reported that the plains were the "Great American Desert." It took many years for settlers to realize that the plains were not a desert, but a fertile, rich land of great possibilities.

Z is for the zebra that eats out of your hand
at the Arbuckle Wilderness, a wild safari land.
And Z is Zebulon Pike, who was rather influential.
He came through Oklahoma, but missed its true potential!

We've crossed Oklahoma, right down to the letter.
And we'll do it again, the Sooner the better.

Sooner Questions

1. What did Sequoyah invent that helped the American Cherokee tribe learn to read?
2. Why were African-American soldiers called "Buffalo" soldiers by the Native Americans of Oklahoma?
3. Where is the National Cowboy Hall of Fame located?
4. What was Chester Gould famous for?
5. When do bald eagles visit Oklahoma?
6. Lake Eufaula has how many miles of lakeshore?
7. Where is Geronimo buried?
8. Who wrote the musical "Oklahoma?"
9. How many different Native American tribes call Oklahoma home?
10. What festival is held in McAlester, Oklahoma every year, and what does it celebrate?
11. Where has Shannon Lucid spent more time than any other woman in the world?
12. Name three astronauts from Oklahoma.
13. Where does mistletoe grow?
14. Which U.S. president approved the plan to make Oklahoma the 46th state in 1906?
15. What stands on the grounds of the state capitol and is the only working one of its kind in any U.S. state?
16. What two Choctaw words were combined to create the name "Oklahoma?" What did each word mean?
17. The town of Quinton was named for Elizabeth Jacob Quinton. How old was she believed to be when she died in 1941?
18. What did Bill Pickett invent?
19. What was the only American town bombed in World War II?
20. What tribe was athelete Jim Thorpe a member of? What three sports did he excel in?

Later Answers

1. "Talking leaves," the Cherokee alphabet with 85 characters
2. For their bravery
3. Oklahoma City, Oklahoma
4. Chester Gould created the comic strip "Dick Tracy"
5. In the winter
6. 600
7. In the Apache cemetery at Fort Sill.
8. Oscar Hammerstein and Richard Rodgers
9. 67
10. The Italian Festival in McAlester celebrates the town's Italian heritage.
11. In space
12. Shannon Lucid, Stuart Roosa, Owen Garriott, William Pogue, and John Harrington

13. At the top of mistletoe trees
14. Theodore Roosevelt
15. An oil well
16. *Okla*, which means "people," and *humma*, which means "red"
17. 115
18. "Bulldogging," now known as steer wrestling
19. Boise, Oklahoma
20. Jim Thorpe was a member of the Sac and Fox tribe. He played professional baseball and football, and won two Olympic gold medals for track in 1912.

Devin Scillian

Author, journalist, and musician Devin Scillian grew up all over the country and all over the world, but it's Oklahoma that he considers home. Formerly an anchor for KFOR-TV in Oklahoma City, Devin now anchors the news for WDIV-TV in Detroit. Devin, his wife Corey, and their four children reside in Grosse Pointe Park, Michigan. Devin's other books include *Cosmo's Moon, Fibblestax, One Nation: America by the Numbers,* and the national bestseller *A is for America: An American Alphabet.*

Kandy Radzinski

Kandy Radzinski received her Masters of Fine Arts from East Texas State University. She taught art at Central Washington State College and the University of Tulsa. Kandy has illustrated children's books, posters, greeting cards, and even a six-foot penguin. Her art has been described as "quirky realism" and can be seen at www.kradzinski.com.

She lives in Tulsa, Oklahoma, with her husband, Mark, her son, Ian, and two Scottie dogs, Mozzie and Kirby. Both Ian and Kandy are second-degree black-belts in Tae Kwon Do.